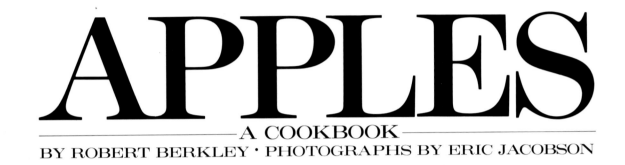

APPLES

A COOKBOOK

BY ROBERT BERKLEY · PHOTOGRAPHS BY ERIC JACOBSON

DESIGN BY LESLEY EHLERS

A FIRESIDE BOOK
PUBLISHED BY SIMON & SCHUSTER INC.
NEW YORK   LONDON   TORONTO   SYDNEY   TOKYO   SINGAPORE

A RUNNING HEADS BOOK

FIRESIDE
Simon & Schuster Building
Rockefeller Center
1230 Avenue of the Americas
New York, New York 10020

FIRESIDE and colophon are registered trademarks
of Simon & Schuster Inc.

APPLES: A COOKBOOK
was conceived and produced by
Running Heads Incorporated
55 West 21 Street
New York, New York 10010

Editor: Linda Greer
Production Manager: Linda Winters
Managing Editor: Lindsey Crittenden

Illustrations by Robbin Gourley

3 5 7 9 10 8 6 4

Library of Congress Cataloging in Publication Data

Berkley, Robert.
Apples : a cookbook / by Robert Berkley; photographs by Eric
Jacobson.
p.   cm.
"A Fireside book."
ISBN 0-671-72902-0
1. Cookery (Apples)   I. Title.
641.6'4—dc20   90-45179
                                                CIP

Typeset by Trufont Typographers, Inc.
Color separations by Hong Kong Scanner Craft Company, Ltd.
Printed and bound in Singapore by Tien Wah Press (Pte.) Ltd.

For Harriet and Larry, Sonja and Zach, Dad and Fran.

AUTHOR'S ACKNOWLEDGEMENTS

I would especially like to thank Caroline Hirsch, Jamie Beecroft, Rita Barol, Jimmy Stanton and all my friends and family at Delta 88 Restaurant and Caroline's at the Seaport for all their love and encouragement, not just on this project but in all my endeavors.

Thanks to Michelle Hauser. Thanks to Sam and Nancy Freitag, William and Mildred Raucher and Loretta and Bruno Hauser. Thanks to all my good friends.

Thanks also to Marta Hallett, Ellen Milionis, Linda Greer, Lindsey Crittenden and Ellie Watson and all the support at Running Heads, as well as to Caroline Herter, Rebecca Verrill and Sydny Miner at Simon & Schuster.

PHOTOGRAPHER'S AND DESIGNER'S ACKNOWLEDGEMENTS

We would like to thank the following people for their support during this project: the Jacobson and Ehlers families, Judy Devine for her inspiration and love, Dexter Samuel for his great energy and smiles while assisting with the photography, Maggie Jones and Leontine Klein for loaning their wonderful props, and Gary Larson for filling the studio with laughter.

Thanks also to Jill Bock, Greg Corso, Beth Farb, Simon Feldman, Robbin Gourley, Kim Kelling, Joey Quintal, Jeffrey Stern, Barbara Vitanza and Myriam Zwierzinska.

Our special thanks to those companies who generously loaned us their beautiful wares: Country Floors, Dean & DeLuca, Fitz and Floyd, Platypus, Jeffrey Weiss New York, and especially Douglas Weiss at Pottery Barn and Pauline Kelly at Zona.

CONTENTS

INTRODUCTION
8

ONE
BREAKFAST
AND BRUNCH

Oatmeal Pancakes with Jonathan
Apples and Pecans
14

Rome Apple, Orange and
Prune Compote
16

Northern Spy Apple Fritters
18

Banana Muffins with
Dried Apples and Apricots
20

Apple-Hazelnut Muffins
20

MacIntosh Apple and
Sausage Pie
22

Winesap Apple Turnovers
24

Spiced Macoun Apple Bread
with Walnuts
26

TWO
SOUPS, SALADS
AND APPETIZERS

Northern Spy Apple
and Butternut Squash Soup
30

MacIntosh Apple and
Blue Cheese Bisque
32

Granny Smith
Apple–Onion Soup
with Celery Root
34

Radicchio, Endive and
Golden Delicious Apple Salad
36

Wilted Greens with
Red Delicious Apples and Bacon
38

Cracked Wheat Salad with
Jonathan Apples and Mint
40

Smoked Turkey and
Gravenstein Apple Salad
42

Rome Apple and
Goat Cheese Tartlets
44

Greening Apple
and Spinach Pâté
46

THREE
MAIN COURSES

Baked Cortland Apples
with Yam Filling
50

Grilled Swordfish with
Lady Apple Butter
52

Brook Trout Baked in
Parchment with
Northern Spy Apples
54

Barbecued Shrimp with
Jonathan Apple and Quince Chutney
56

Red Snapper with
Empire Apples and Walnuts
58

Turkey Potpie with
Newtown Pippins and Onions
60

Duck Breasts with Crab Apples
62

Chicken and
Cortland Apple Couscous
64

Pork Chops with Rome Apple
and Rosemary Stuffing
66

Spareribs with
Applesauce Glaze
68

Grilled Veal Chops
and Granny Smith Apples
70

CONTENTS

FOUR
ACCOMPANIMENTS

Braised Red Cabbage with
Northern Spy Apples
74

Caramelized Greening Apples
and Pearl Onions
74

Fresh Golden Delicious
Apple–Walnut Relish
76

Ginger Crab Apple Applesauce
76

Carrot, Parsnip and
Granny Smith Apple Coleslaw
78

Three-Apple Apple Butter
80

FIVE
DESSERTS

Cran-Apple Pie
84

Calvados Soufflé
86

Jonathan Apples Poached
in Red Wine
88

MacIntosh Apple Cobblers
with Vanilla Ice Cream
90

Winesap Apple Pudding
92

Candied Lady Apples
94

Granny Smith Apple Sorbet
96

Golden Delicious Apple
and Cinnamon Ice Cream
98

Macoun Apple Pie
100

Golden Delicious Apples with
Caramel and Cookies
102

Baked Rome Apples
with Cointreau
104

Jonathan Apple Dumplings
106

Empire Apple and Pear Tarts
108

SIX
BEVERAGES

Apple-Apricot Smoothie
112

Apple-Cranberry Iced Tea
112

Hot Buttered Cider
114

Applejack Punch
114

Calvados Spritzer
116

Apple Cider Spritzer
116

RECIPE LIST
118

RECIPE LIST BY APPLE
OR APPLE PRODUCT
118

SOURCES
120

INTRODUCTION

Versatile, enduring, delicate—these qualities describe the apple as a concept as well as a food. The apple is as much a part of the iconography of cooking and folk culture as a stove, a pot or a ladle; so much so that the mere mention of, say, apple pie is often enough to evoke images and memories that are inextricably associated with the pie: a picnic, a birthday, a family holiday gathering.

When I thought of doing my next cookbook these associations immediately suggested a collection of traditional recipes, but with a slight twist: recipes from *different* traditions, like Southern American, Slavic and British among others.

Several factors contribute to the making of a traditional cuisine: regional ingredients, economic conditions and their effect on cooking and storage facilities and, sometimes, religious restrictions. Another contributing factor is the passage of time. The nuances of a dish can vary from one occasion to the next or from one generation to the next. This is natural. But what makes a dish traditional is if its form remains constant through its many executions. In fact many cultures share similar forms for their national dishes, and only vary in their ingredients. Consider, for example, the similarities between a tortilla and a pita, a ravioli and a pierogi, or a blintz and a crepe.

As an American chef what draws me to the kitchen is the pursuit of the roots and development of American dishes. The melting-pot principle that so sharply affects so much of our culture is most evident in our cooking. Coleslaw, hamburgers, omelets—these dishes are Dutch, English and French in origin. How these dishes became adapted to American culture goes beyond the old story of settlers from these countries bringing their national foods with them. An unusual evolution occurs when somebody attempts a dish not native to their culture. They attach their own innate sensibilities and come up with something slightly different. It is an issue of assimilation, like the way an immigrant named Sven becomes Steven, or Johannes becomes John. The old and new characteristics merge and form a new landscape of language, arts and food.

The apple is a natural representative of American cooking and culture. It is a common ingredient throughout most of the world's cooking, so international dishes appear to be right at home. It is an ingredient that can be manipulated in many ways, maintain its identity and still yield itself to its intended use. It can be sautéed, baked, fried, grilled or just sliced. It works wonderfully with meats, in salads, in desserts or by itself. An apple is a fruit that has a thin but tough skin, a very tough core, inedible seeds, and firm, fibrous meat that accounts for about 90 percent of its composition. Depending on the variety, apples can be sweet, juicy, tart, sour, even

cooked, the tartness is mellowed but the texture tends to dry a little, easily remedied by adding sugar to such recipes as apple pie. The Rome (or Rome Beauty) is large and deep red, almost perfectly round. It is primarily a cooking apple, with less flavor when eaten raw. But when baked, a richly mellow, almost savory flavor emerges. The Northern Spy is large and pale yellow-green with thin pink stripes coming out of the center. It is a beautiful apple with a gentle, tart flavor. It is a great apple for salads or for sautéing. One of my favorite farmer's market discoveries is the Winesap. This apple has a dense red skin with black-and-white freckles and very firm, white meat. It is most succulent and juicy, almost wine-flavored. I have to buy more than I need because I can't resist them and eventually eat some before I reach my kitchen.

Who is to say which apples do best for which dishes? I have been told, and have read, not to cook with Granny Smiths, just to eat them raw. But I have made delicious apple pies with thinly sliced Granny Smiths, a little sugar and a pinch of salt. I have heard not to bake MacIntoshes, but they seem perfect in apple cobblers. While it is true that there are some apples that do better than others in some situations, only through experimentation can you determine which can successfully substitute for others in any given recipe.

The following general guidelines should help in deciding which apples to try substituting for others, but don't be afraid to experiment with apples outside of these categories. Of the apples used in this book, Cortlands, Empires, Granny Smiths, Gravensteins, Jonathans, Lady apples, Macouns, MacIntoshes, Newtown Pippins and Northern Spies are all considered all-purpose apples, suitable for cooking or eating raw. Within this group, some are often better than others for certain applications: Cortlands, as in Baked Cortland Apples with Yam Filling, are great for baking whole (especially in the microwave) because they maintain their shape; Jonathans and MacIntoshes can be a good choice for quick-cooking methods or for applesauce or soup, like MacIntosh Apple and Blue Cheese Bisque, because they tend to lose their shape; and the Northern Spy's flavor develops well when cooked, but Gravensteins taste better raw. Only two of the apples used in this book are generally regarded as best eaten raw: the Red and Golden Delicious. Three are most often cooked before eating: Crab Apples, Greenings and Romes. One other factor to keep in mind when looking for an apple substitute is flavor—tart substitutes for tart, sweet for sweet, and so on. For instance Greenings and Granny Smiths, both very tart, could replace each other in a recipe; Macouns and MacIntoshes, which are relatives, are very similar in taste; and Winesaps might be suitable stand-ins for Jonathans as they both have a savory flavor.

The only rule is that there are no rules. Once you are familiar with the different varieties of apples and apple products and their properties, you will be able to elicit the response you want and achieve your culinary goals.

OATMEAL PANCAKES WITH JONATHAN APPLES AND PECANS

1½ cups oatmeal
1½ cups boiling water
1 egg
1 cup flour
2 tablespoons baking powder
pinch of salt
¼ cup sugar
1 cup milk
¼ cup melted butter
3 Jonathan apples, peeled, cored and
  chopped
½ cup pecan pieces
2 tablespoons butter

· Combine oatmeal and boiling water. Let stand 5 minutes.
· Add egg, flour, baking powder, salt and sugar. Mix.
· Stir in milk, melted butter, apples and pecans.
· Melt 2 tablespoons butter in a large, flat skillet or griddle over medium heat.
· When the butter begins to crackle, spoon on pancake batter to desired size. Gently flip pancakes when bubbles form around the edges and in the center. Cook for another minute and serve with maple syrup.

Makes about 15 3-inch pancakes.
Preparation time: 45 minutes.

ROME APPLE, ORANGE AND PRUNE COMPOTE

1 orange
¼ cup sugar (or less to taste)
6 pitted prunes
1 Rome apple, peeled, cored and
   diced
2 ounces dark rum or cognac

· Peel orange and cut into sections, carefully removing membranes and white pith. Cut peel into thin strips.
· In a heavy skillet, dissolve sugar in 1 cup water. Boil for 4 to 5 minutes. Add orange peel and prunes. Continue boiling for another 4 to 5 minutes.
· Lower heat to a simmer. Add apple and orange sections. Cook until apple is tender, adding more water if necessary. Remove from heat and add rum.

Serves 2.
Preparation time: 25 minutes.

NORTHERN SPY
APPLE FRITTERS

¾ cup yellow cornmeal
½ cup all-purpose flour
2 tablespoons baking powder
6 tablespoons sugar
pinch of salt
1 egg
½ cup milk
1½ cups vegetable oil (for frying)
1 Northern Spy apple, peeled, cored
   and chopped
2 tablespoons vegetable oil
confectioners' sugar (for garnish)

· Combine all dry ingredients (except confectioners' sugar). Add liquid ingredients (except 1½ cups oil) one at a time, stirring between additions. Mix in apple. Let batter sit for 10 minutes.
· In a 1-quart saucepan over medium-high heat, heat the oil until it crackles, not quite to the smoking point. Take precautionary measures for using hot oil!
· Drop batter into the oil 1 tablespoon at a time (get close so the oil doesn't splash). Fry only 2 or 3 fritters at a time—don't crowd the pan.
· Flip the fritters over and remove onto a paper towel when golden brown. Sprinkle with confectioners' sugar and serve.

Makers 15 to 18 fritters.
Preparation time: 40 minutes.

BANANA MUFFINS WITH DRIED APPLES AND APRICOTS

½ cup all-purpose flour
½ cup whole wheat flour
2 tablespoons baking powder
¼ cup sugar
1 egg
2 tablespoons unsalted butter, melted and cooled
½ cup warm milk
1 banana, sliced
¼ cup chopped dried apples
¼ cup chopped dried apricots
pinch of salt
1 teaspoon vanilla extract

· Preheat oven to 350°.
· Combine flours, baking powder and sugar. Add egg, butter and milk, and mix. Stir in the banana, apples and apricots. Add salt and vanilla.
· Fill 4 cups of a nonstick muffin pan (or regular muffin pan with paper liners) with the batter.
· Bake for 8 to 10 minutes, until a toothpick inserted in the center comes out clean.

Serves 4.
Preparation time: 20 minutes.

APPLE-HAZELNUT MUFFINS

½ cup hazelnuts, ground in blender to a coarse flour
½ cup all-purpose flour
2 tablespoons baking powder
¼ cup sugar
1 egg
2 tablespoons unsalted butter, melted and cooled
½ cup warm milk
1 teaspoon vanilla extract
pinch of salt
½ cup chopped dried apples

· Preheat oven to 350°.
· Combine hazelnuts, flour, baking powder and sugar. Add egg, butter, milk, vanilla, salt and apples. Let stand 10 minutes.
· Fill 4 cups of a nonstick muffin pan (or regular muffin pan with paper liners) with the batter.
· Bake 8 to 10 minutes, until a toothpick inserted in the center comes out clean.

Serves 4.
Preparation time: 30 minutes.

MACINTOSH APPLE AND SAUSAGE PIE

4 tablespoons cold unsalted butter,
  cut into small pieces
½ cup all-purpose flour
½ pound sweet sausage
1 tablespoon butter
1 MacIntosh apple, peeled, cored and
  diced
2 egg yolks
1 whole egg
1 cup heavy cream
salt
½ cup shredded sharp cheddar cheese

· Preheat oven to 350°.
· Combine 4 tablespoons cold butter with the flour and a pinch of salt. Mix with fingertips until butter is almost entirely incorporated and mixture has the consistency of coarse bread crumbs. Add 1 to 2 tablespoons cold water to bind. Refrigerate for 30 minutes.
· Remove the sausage from its casing and crumble. In a skillet over medium-high heat, sauté the sausage until cooked through. Drain well. Set aside.
· In a separate skillet, heat 1 tablespoon butter and sauté the apple for a minute, just until softened. Set aside.
· Combine egg yolks and egg with cream and a pinch of salt. Set aside.
· Roll out dough and press into a 9-inch pie tin. Place sausage in bottom of pie tin. Arrange apple on top of sausage and distribute cheese evenly over apple. Pour egg mixture over all. Bake for 50 minutes to 1 hour, until pie is somewhat firm when touched. Cool for a few minutes and serve warm.

Serves 4 to 6.
Preparation time: 1 hour 45 minutes.

WINESAP APPLE TURNOVERS

3 tablespoons butter
2 Winesap apples, peeled, cored and
  diced
4 6-inch circles frozen puff pastry,
  thawed
1 egg, beaten with a little water

· Preheat oven to 350°.
· Melt 2 tablespoons butter in a skillet and sauté apples for a minute,
  just until softened. Cool. Grease a
  cookie sheet with remaining butter.
· Arrange the apples in the center of
  the 4 pastry circles. Fold the circles
  in half and pinch the edges closed
  with your fingertips or a fork.
· Brush the egg sparingly on the tops
  of the turnovers. Place on greased
  cookie sheet and bake for 8 to 10
  minutes until the pastry has risen
  and is golden brown. Serve warm.

Serves 4.
Preparation time: 25 minutes.

SPICED MACOUN APPLE BREAD WITH WALNUTS

2 tablespoons butter
1 Macoun apple, peeled, cored and
    diced
¼ cup walnuts, chopped
6 eggs, separated
6 tablespoons sugar
2 cups whole wheat flour, sifted
½ teaspoon nutmeg
½ teaspoon cinnamon

· Preheat oven to 350°.
· Melt 1 tablespoon butter in a skillet, and sauté apple and walnuts
  until apple is softened. Set aside to
  cool.
· Beat egg whites until stiff.
· Combine sugar and egg yolks.
  Gradually fold beaten egg whites
  into yolks. Fold in flour. Add apples, walnuts and spices, being
  careful not to overmix or batter will
  deflate.
· With remaining butter, grease a
  8- × 4- × 3-inch loaf pan. Gently pour batter into pan and bake for
  30 to 40 minutes, until a toothpick
  inserted in the center comes out
  clean.

Serves 6 to 8.
Preparation time: 1 hour 15 minutes.

26

TWO • SOUPS, SALADS AND APPETIZERS

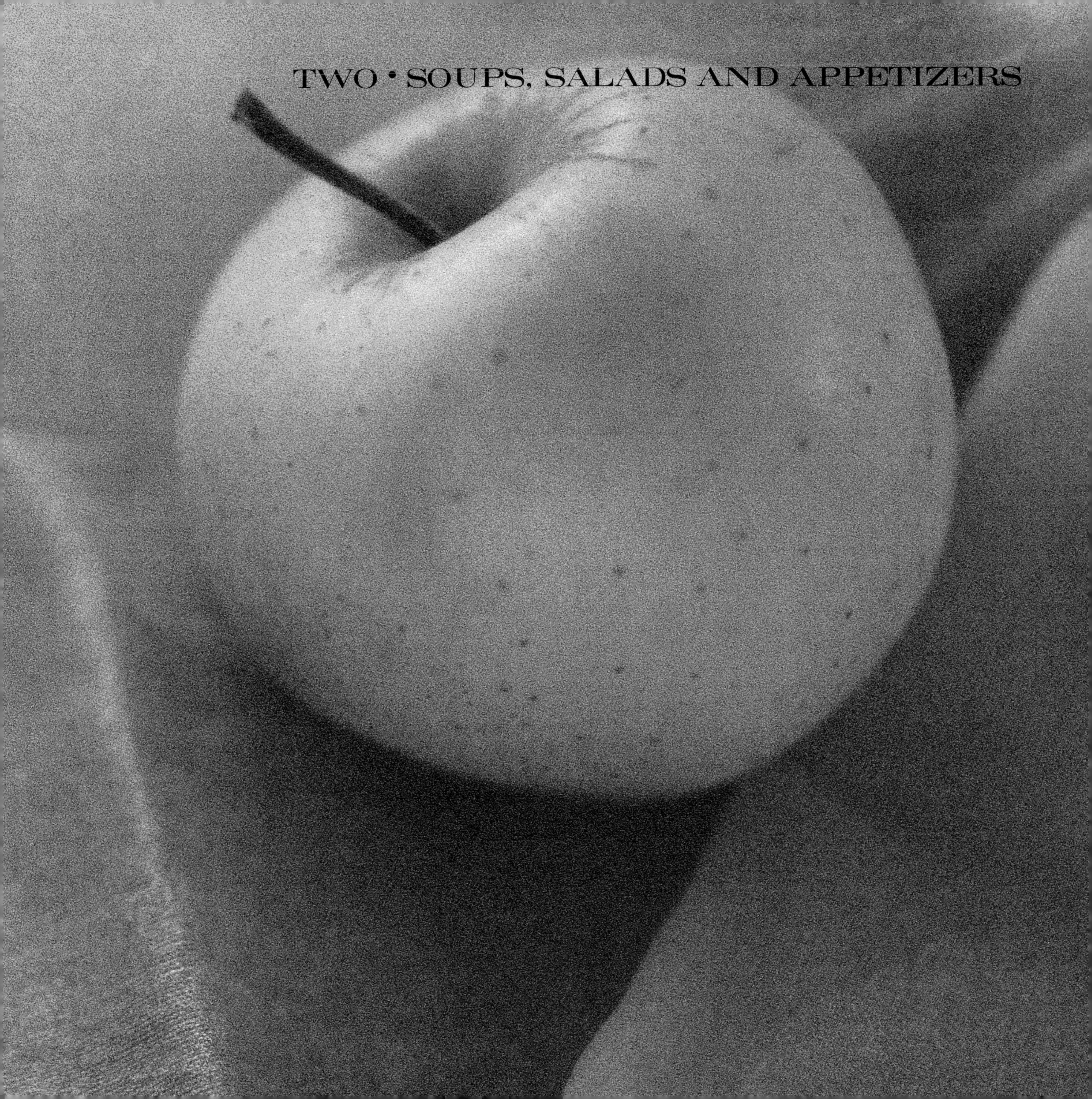

NORTHERN SPY APPLE AND BUTTERNUT SQUASH SOUP

VEGETABLE STOCK:
2 tablespoons vegetable oil
3 carrots, finely chopped
3–4 celery stalks, finely chopped
1 large Spanish onion, finely chopped
1 tablespoon whole black peppercorns
3–4 bay leaves
1 bunch parsley

SOUP:
2–3 Northern Spy apples, peeled,
    cored and coarsely chopped
1 butternut squash, peeled, seeded
    and coarsely chopped
salt

· To make vegetable stock, heat oil in a 4-quart pot over medium heat. When hot, add vegetables, peppercorns, bay leaves and parsley. Sauté until vegetables are softened and begin to brown (about 20 minutes), being careful not to burn them.
· Add 2½ quarts cold water. Raise heat to high. Bring to a full boil, and then lower to a simmer. Cook for about 45 minutes, until stock is rich and flavorful. Strain and discard vegetables.
· To make soup, return 1½ quarts strained stock to a simmer. Add the apples and the squash. Cook until tender, about 45 minutes.
· Mash squash with a potato masher or force through a strainer if smooth puree is desired. Season with salt to taste. Add water if too thick; simmer longer if too thin.

Serves 6.
Preparation time: 2 hours 15 minutes.

MACINTOSH APPLE AND BLUE CHEESE BISQUE

1 tablespoon unsalted butter
2 MacIntosh apples, peeled, cored
    and coarsely chopped
1½ cups milk
5–6 ounces blue cheese
salt and pepper

· In a 2-quart saucepan over medium
  heat, melt the butter and sauté the
  apples until very soft.
· Add the milk and lower the heat.
· When the milk starts to scald
  around the edges begin adding the
  cheese, bit by bit, stirring constantly. (The milk may begin to
  separate at this point; just keep
  adding the cheese and stirring.)
  When all the cheese has been incorporated, add salt and pepper to
  taste.

Serves 2.
Preparation time: 30 minutes.

GRANNY SMITH APPLE—ONION SOUP WITH CELERY ROOT

2 medium onions, coarsely chopped
2 large red potatoes, diced (skin
  optional)
3 Granny Smith apples, peeled,
  cored and chopped
1 medium celery root, peeled and
  diced
2 tablespoons vegetable oil
1 gallon chicken stock
salt and pepper
chopped chives for garnish (optional)

· In a large pot, sauté onions, potatoes, apples and celery root in
  the oil.
· When the onions are soft, add the
  chicken stock. Bring to a boil, then
  lower to a simmer and cook for
  about 40 minutes, until all the vegetables are very soft.
· Force through a sieve or puree in a
  blender. Return to pot and reheat.
  Add salt and pepper to taste. Serve
  garnished with chopped chives if
  desired.

Serves 10.
Preparation time: 1 hour 15 minutes.

RADICCHIO, ENDIVE AND GOLDEN DELICIOUS APPLE SALAD

1 head radicchio, leaves separated
2 heads Belgian endive, chopped
1 Golden Delicious apple, peeled,
  cored and diced
¼ cup sour cream

· Arrange radicchio on 4 plates.
· Toss endive and apple together, and
  distribute evenly on the radicchio.
· Place a dollop of sour cream in the
  center of each salad.

Serves 4.
Preparation time: 10 minutes.

WILTED GREENS WITH RED DELICIOUS APPLES AND BACON

1 bunch watercress
1 bunch dandelion greens
1 small red onion, sliced very thin
1 Red Delicious apple, peeled, cored
  and sliced thin
6 ounces bacon, cooked crisp,
  drained well and coarsely
  crumbled
1 lemon

· In a 2-quart saucepan bring 2 cups water to a boil. Fit a strainer or colander on top of the pan, over but not in the water. Toss watercress and dandelion greens together in the strainer; cover and steam for about 2 to 3 minutes, checking frequently so the greens don't overcook.
· When greens are just wilted, arrange on 4 plates.
· Arrange onion slices on greens, and top with apple slices and crumbled bacon.
· Squeeze lemon juice over each salad.

Serves 4.
Preparation time: 15 minutes.

CRACKED WHEAT SALAD WITH JONATHAN APPLES AND MINT

¾ cup cracked wheat (bulgur)
¼ cup shelled pecans
2 Jonathan apples, peeled, cored and
  diced
2–3 plum tomatoes, seeded and
  diced
1 large sprig fresh mint, finely
  chopped
salt and pepper
1 tablespoon extra virgin olive oil
juice of 1 lemon

· Soak cracked wheat in ¾ cup hot
  water for 30 minutes or until tender. Drain off any excess water.
· Preheat oven to 350°.
· While wheat is soaking, place the
  pecans in an ovenproof skillet and
  toast for about 5 minutes, until
  dark brown and aromatic. Cool.
· Combine nuts, wheat, apples, tomatoes and mint and season generously with salt and pepper. Sprinkle
  with olive oil and lemon juice.

Serves 2.
Preparation time: 40 minutes.

SMOKED TURKEY AND GRAVENSTEIN APPLE SALAD

VINAIGRETTE:
2 tablespoons cider vinegar
6 tablespoons olive oil
1 tablespoon Dijon mustard
salt and pepper

SALAD:
1 bunch watercress
1 carrot, peeled and finely julienned
16 cherry tomatoes
10 ounces smoked turkey, coarsely
  chopped
2 cups vegetable oil
4 Gravenstein apples, peeled, cored
  and quartered

· Whisk together cider vinegar, olive oil and mustard, and add salt and pepper to taste. Refrigerate until needed.
· Arrange watercress, carrot, tomatoes and turkey on 4 salad plates.
· Heat the vegetable oil in a heavy, 1-quart skillet. When hot (about 350°), fry the apples until golden brown. Remove from oil and place on paper towels to drain. Arrange on the plates. Serve with the vinaigrette.

Serves 4.
Preparation time: 25 minutes.

ROME APPLE AND GOAT CHEESE TARTLETS

½ cup cold unsalted butter, cut into
    small pieces
1 cup all-purpose flour
pinch of salt
1 Rome apple, peeled, cored and
    thinly sliced
½ pound goat cheese

· Preheat oven to 350°.
· Combine butter, flour and salt with fingertips until butter is mostly incorporated and the mixture has the consistency of coarse bread crumbs. Add 2 to 3 tablespoons cold water to bind. Refrigerate for 30 minutes. Roll out and press into eight 2-inch tart shells. (Excess dough can be wrapped and refrigerated for up to 2 weeks.)
· Arrange 2 or 3 slices of apple in each tart shell. Place shells on a cookie sheet and bake for about 20 minutes, until crusts are golden brown. Let stand until cool enough to handle.
· Place 1 ounce of cheese in each tart and bake 5 minutes, until cheese softens and begins to brown. Serve warm.

Makes 8 tartlets.
Preparation time: 1 hour 15 minutes.

GREENING APPLE AND SPINACH PÂTÉ

2 Greening apples, peeled, cored and
 coarsely chopped
2–3 tablespoons unsalted butter
1 pound fresh spinach, washed
 thoroughly and stems removed
2 eggs
1¼ cups walnuts, ground in blender
 to a coarse flour
¾ cup fresh unseasoned bread
 crumbs
salt and pepper

· Sauté apples in butter until soft.
 Remove apples and set aside.
· Sauté spinach in remaining butter
 until wilted and drain well. Puree
 in blender or food processor.
· Beat together eggs, walnuts, spinach, apples and bread crumbs. Add
 salt and pepper to taste.
· Lay a large piece of plastic wrap on
 a table or counter and pour the mixture lengthwise down the center of
 the plastic. Roll the plastic around
 the mixture to form a log, approx-
 imately 3 inches in diameter. Tie
 the ends closed with string and refrigerate for at least 1 hour. When
 thoroughly chilled, remove pâté
 from the refrigerator and reshape
 log (leaving it wrapped); it should
 be as smooth and cylindrical as
 possible.
· Fill a large skillet or shallow saucepan with enough water to cover the
 pâté and place over medium heat.
 Bring to a simmer and reduce heat
 so water is just barely moving.
 Place the pâté in the water and
 poach for 30 to 45 minutes,
 until firm.
· Remove from water and refrigerate
 overnight. Peel off plastic wrap and
 slice to serve.

Serves 4 to 6.
Preparation time: 2 hours 15 minutes, set overnight.

THREE • MAIN COURSES

BAKED CORTLAND APPLES WITH YAM FILLING

1 tablespoon vegetable oil
1 yam, peeled and diced
1 small red bell pepper, diced
1 medium onion, diced
¼ teaspoon fresh chopped or dried thyme
salt and pepper
2 slices firm white bread, crumbled
1 14-ounce can whole peeled tomatoes
4 Cortland apples, cored and hollowed out

· Preheat oven to 400°.
· Heat oil over medium heat and sauté yam, pepper and onion with thyme until soft. Add salt and pepper to taste. Set aside.
· Combine pepper and onion mixture with bread and 3 or 4 tablespoons of juice from the can of tomatoes.
· Stuff mixture into the apples. Place the tomatoes and remaining juice into an ovenproof, non-reactive skillet and arrange the apples on top. Bake for 25 to 30 minutes, until apples are tender.

Serves 4.
Preparation time: 1 hour.

GRILLED SWORDFISH WITH LADY APPLE BUTTER

¼ cup unsalted butter, softened
1 Lady apple, peeled, cored and
    finely chopped
salt and pepper
2 7–8-ounce pieces of swordfish
2 tablespoons olive or vegetable oil

· Preheat grill to high following manufacturer's instructions. (Or use a broiler if a grill is unavailable.)
· Using a small piece of the butter in a skillet, sauté the apple until tender.
· Combine the softened butter, cooked apple and salt and pepper to taste. Roll into a log in foil, plastic wrap or the butter wrapper, and re-frigerate until hardened.
· Rub the swordfish with the oil and some salt and pepper. Place on the hottest spot on the grill (or under the broiler). Cook for about 3 to 4 minutes; turn 90 degrees with a spatula, and cook for another 3 to 4 minutes. Flip swordfish over onto a cooler spot on the grill, and cook for another 3 to 4 minutes.
· Place the fish on 2 plates and slice the cold butter onto the fish.

Serves 2.
Preparation time: 30 minutes.

BROOK TROUT BAKED IN PARCHMENT WITH NORTHERN SPY APPLES

2 whole brook trout, cleaned, heads
  and fins removed
2 pieces parchment paper cut into
  12-inch circles
4 slices lemon
4 sprigs fresh or 1 teaspoon dried
  thyme
1 Northern Spy apple, peeled, cored,
  quartered and sliced
2–3 scallions, chopped
2 tablespoons unsalted butter
salt and pepper

· Preheat oven to 400°.
· Place each trout, opened, in the
  center of each piece of parchment
  paper.
· Place 2 slices of lemon, 2 sprigs of
  fresh thyme (or ½ teaspoon dried
  thyme), half of the sliced apple, half
  of the chopped scallions and 1 tablespoon butter inside each trout. Add
  salt and pepper to taste.
· Close up trouts. Fold paper in half
  over fish to form a semicircle, and
  make small overlapping folds along
  the rim to seal.
· Place fish in paper in an 11- × 14-
  inch baking pan, and bake for 20
  minutes. Serve inside paper.

Serves 2.
Preparation time: 35 minutes.

BARBECUED SHRIMP WITH JONATHAN APPLE AND QUINCE CHUTNEY

CHUTNEY:

¼ cup sugar
½ cup dried apricots, chopped
5–6 pitted prunes, chopped
¼ cup golden raisins
2 Jonathan apples, peeled, cored and
    coarsely chopped
¼ cup quince preserves
¼ cup bourbon

SHRIMP:

12 medium-sized shrimp, peeled and
    deveined

· In a heavy skillet dissolve sugar in 1 cup water over medium heat. Add apricots, prunes and raisins, and cook for 4 to 5 minutes.
· Add apples and preserves. Cook until apples are tender. Remove from heat and add bourbon. Cool.
· Preheat grill to high following manufacturer's instructions. (May be broiled if a grill is unavailable.)
· Skewer shrimp. Brush chutney (including the chunks of fruit) generously on all sides of shrimp and place on the hottest spot on the grill (or under the broiler). Turn occasionally, brushing the shrimp with more chutney. Cook until shrimp are firm to the touch, about 6 minutes. Store extra chutney in a glass jar in the refrigerator for up to 4 weeks.

Serves 2. (Makes 1½ to 2 cups chutney.)
Preparation time: 45 minutes.

RED SNAPPER WITH EMPIRE APPLES AND WALNUTS

⅓ cup walnut pieces
2 7–8-ounce red snapper fillets
salt and pepper
¼ cup all-purpose flour
3 tablespoons vegetable oil
2 Empire apples, peeled, cored and
   chopped
2–3 leaves fresh sage, chopped, or ½
   teaspoon dried sage (optional)

· Preheat oven to 400°.
· Place the walnuts in an ovenproof skillet and toast in the oven for about 5 minutes, until darkened a shade and aromatic. Remove from oven, cool and set aside.
· Lightly dust the fish with salt, pepper and flour.
· Place an ovenproof skillet with 2 tablespoons oil over medium-high heat. When oil is hot, place the fish, flesh side down, in the pan. Lower the heat.
· When the fish is golden brown, turn it over and place it in the oven for about 5 to 6 minutes.
· In a separate skillet, heat the remaining tablespoon of oil. Add apples, toasted walnuts, sage (if desired) and salt and pepper. Sauté for a few minutes until the apples are tender.
· Remove fish from the oven and place on 2 plates. Spoon apples and nuts onto the fish.

Serves 2.
Preparation time: 20 minutes.

TURKEY POTPIE WITH NEWTOWN PIPPINS AND ONIONS

2 cups all-purpose flour
1 cup unsalted butter, cut into small
    pieces
pinch of salt
2 tablespoons vegetable oil
1 large Spanish onion, chopped
½ pound cooked turkey, coarsely
    chopped
¾ cup white wine
¼ cup heavy cream
¼ cup yellow cornmeal
2 sprigs fresh mint, chopped
    (optional)
salt and pepper
2 Newtown Pippins, peeled, cored
    and chopped
1 egg, beaten

· Preheat oven to 350°.
· In a bowl, combine flour, butter and a pinch of salt. Mix together with fingertips until butter is mostly incorporated and mixture has the consistency of coarse bread crumbs. Add 4 to 5 tablespoons cold water to bind. Form into a patty and refrigerate for 30 minutes.
· While dough chills, make the filling. Heat the vegetable oil in a large skillet over medium heat. Add the onion and cook until soft. Add the turkey. Cook for 2 to 3 minutes until turkey softens. Add wine and reduce for 2 to 3 minutes. Add cream. Bring to a boil and reduce 2 to 3 minutes. Add cornmeal, mint (if desired), salt, pepper and apples. Cook for another 5 minutes.
· Fill 4 individual 5-inch round casserole dishes with the filling. Roll out dough and cut into the shape of the dishes. Place on top of the turkey filling, and brush with the beaten egg.
· Bake for 30 to 40 minutes until crust is golden brown.

Serves 4.
Preparation time: 1 hour 30 minutes.

DUCK BREASTS
WITH CRAB APPLES

1–2 tablespoons vegetable oil
2 boneless duck breasts, trimmed
  of fat
2 tablespoons all-purpose flour
4 Crab Apples, quartered and cored
1–2 sprigs fresh thyme
salt and pepper

· Preheat oven to 400°.
· In an ovenproof skillet, heat the oil
to the smoking point. Dust the
breasts lightly with flour and place
in the hot skillet skin side down.
Cook for 1 to 2 minutes until
golden brown; turn over; reduce
heat and add the apple quarters and
thyme. Sprinkle salt, pepper and 2
to 3 tablespoons water over all
ingredients.
· Place the skillet in the oven for 5 to
6 minutes. Duck breasts should be
somewhat firm—medium rare to
medium—and apples should be soft
and wilted.
· Slice breasts and arrange on plates
with apples, thyme and remaining
juices from the pan.

Serves 2.
Preparation time: 15 minutes.

CHICKEN AND CORTLAND APPLE COUSCOUS

2 cups coarsely chopped cooked
  chicken
2 cups dry couscous
2½ cups boiling chicken stock
½ cup golden raisins
½ cup toasted slivered almonds
2 Cortland apples, peeled, cored and
  coarsely chopped
¼ cup unsalted butter, cut into small
  pieces
½ teaspoon ground coriander seeds
¼ teaspoon ground cinnamon
⅛ teaspoon ground cloves

· Preheat oven to 400°.
· Combine all ingredients in an
  9- × 13- × 2-inch glass baking
  pan. Cover with foil and bake for
  25 minutes.

Serves 4.
Preparation time: 45 minutes.

PORK CHOPS WITH ROME APPLE AND ROSEMARY STUFFING

2 leeks, white part only, split
    lengthwise, washed and chopped,
    or 1 medium Spanish onion, finely
    diced
¼ cup vegetable oil
1 medium-sized Idaho potato,
    grated, with skin
1 sprig fresh rosemary, leaves
    removed and finely chopped, or ½
    teaspoon dried rosemary
1 Rome apple, peeled, cored and
    diced
1 slice firm white or whole wheat
    bread, crumbled
salt and pepper
8 pork chops (preferably loin chops)

· In a large skillet, sauté the leeks in
half of the vegetable oil until soft.
Add the potato and rosemary.
· Add the apple and continue sautéing. You may need to add some water if the mixture is too dry. When
the potato is tender, add the bread
and salt and pepper to taste. Lower
heat to keep the stuffing warm.
· In a separate skillet (you may need
2 for all 8 chops), sauté the pork
chops in remaining oil for 6 to 8
minutes per side, making sure the
oil is hot before you add the chops.
Serve with a spoonful of the
stuffing.

Serves 4.
Preparation time: 35 minutes.

SPARERIBS WITH APPLESAUCE GLAZE

2 racks pork spareribs, skin removed
    from bone side
salt and pepper
1½ cups applesauce

· Preheat oven to 350°.
· Season ribs generously with salt and pepper on both sides. Place ribs, standing up on their sides, in an ovenproof skillet. Add 1 cup of water. Cover with aluminum foil and bake for 2 to 2½ hours. Remove carefully from oven and let cool at least 2 hours or overnight.
· When the ribs are cooled, cut into individual pieces.
· Preheat grill to high following manufacturer's instructions. (May be broiled if a grill is unavailable.)
· Brush ribs with applesauce and place on the grill (or under the broiler). Turn ribs, continuing to apply applesauce with a brush, until meat is tender and heated throughout, about 10 minutes.

Serves 4 to 6.
Preparation time: 2 hours 30 minutes, plus cooling time, plus 15 minutes. (It is best to begin this recipe the day before or at least 6 hours prior to serving.)

GRILLED VEAL CHOPS AND GRANNY SMITH APPLES

2 10-ounce veal chops
2 tablespoons vegetable oil
salt and pepper
2 tablespoons unsalted butter,
    softened
2 Granny Smith apples, sliced
    crosswise into ½-inch rounds (do
    not peel or core)

· Preheat grill to high following
  manufacturer's instructions. (Or use
  a broiler if a grill is unavailable.)
· Rub veal chops with vegetable oil
  and season with salt and pepper.
  Place on the hottest spot on the
  grill (or under the broiler).
· Rub softened butter on apple slices
  and sprinkle with salt and pepper.
  Place on the coolest spot on the
  grill (or under the broiler).
· Turn veal chops every few minutes
  until they are firm to the touch,
  about 10 minutes.
· Turn apple slices until golden
  brown on both sides and tender.
  Veal chops and apples should be
  ready at about the same time if they
  are begun together.

Serves 2.
Preparation time: 20 minutes.

FOUR • ACCOMPANIMENTS

BRAISED RED CABBAGE WITH NORTHERN SPY APPLES

2 tablespoons vegetable oil
2 small red onions, peeled, halved
    and sliced
1 small head red cabbage, outer
    leaves removed, quartered and
    sliced
2 Northern Spy apples, peeled, cored
    and julienned
2 tablespoons caraway seeds
2 cups dry vermouth
salt and pepper

· Heat the oil in a large skillet. Add
  the onions and cabbage and sauté
  for a few seconds. Add the apples
  and caraway seeds. Toss ingredients
  together.
· Remove from heat; add the vermouth and return to heat. Bring to
  a simmer; cover and cook for about
  6 to 7 minutes until cabbage is tender but still a bit crunchy. Add salt
  and pepper to taste.

Serves 8.
Preparation time: 30 minutes.

CARAMELIZED GREENING APPLES AND PEARL ONIONS

2 tablespoons unsalted butter
1 cup fresh pearl onions, peeled
salt and pepper
2 Greening apples, peeled, cored and
    quartered

· In a heavy skillet over medium
  heat, melt butter and sauté onions
  until translucent. Add salt and pepper to taste.
· Cut each apple quarter in half cross-
  wise and add to the pan. Cook,
  tossing occasionally, until golden
  brown. Lower heat if necessary.

Serves 4 to 6.
Preparation time: 15 minutes.

FRESH GOLDEN DELICIOUS APPLE–WALNUT RELISH

1 cup shelled walnuts
2 Golden Delicious apples, peeled, cored and diced
½ cup sweet red wine

· Preheat oven to 350°.
· Place walnuts in a pan and toast for 5 minutes until dark brown and aromatic. Cool and chop.
· Combine all ingredients. Best when served the next day.

Serves 6 to 8.
Preparation time: 15 minutes.

GINGER CRAB APPLE APPLESAUCE

3 pounds Crab Apples, stems removed
1 4–6 ounce piece fresh ginger, peeled and coarsely chopped, or 2–3 tablespoons ground ginger
2 cups cranberry juice

· Place the apples in a heavy-bottomed, 6-quart pot (copper is best.)
· Add the fresh ginger. If you are using ground ginger, wait until the end to add it.
· Add cranberry juice.
· Cook on low heat for 45 minutes to 1 hour, stirring frequently. You may need to add a little water.
· When the apples are cooked through and very soft, force the "meat" through a sieve or stainless steel strainer into a bowl. Add ground ginger now if using. (Taste the applesauce as you add the ginger, as the intensity of dried spices can vary widely depending on their age, the brand, even the light and heat conditions under which they are stored.)
· Allow to cool. Serve warm or cold.

Serves 15.
Preparation time: 1 hour 15 minutes.

CARROT, PARSNIP AND GRANNY SMITH APPLE COLESLAW

4 carrots, shredded
3 small parsnips, shredded
2 Granny Smith apples, peeled,
  cored and finely chopped
¼ head red cabbage, shredded
1 small red onion, thinly sliced
  (optional)
2 tablespoons chopped parsley
½ cup mayonnaise
1 tablespoon sugar
salt and pepper

· Combine carrots, parsnips, apples,
  cabbage, onion and parsley.
· Add mayonnaise, sugar, and salt
  and pepper to taste. Mix all ingredients well.

Serves 6 to 8.
Preparation time: 45 minutes.

THREE-APPLE
APPLE BUTTER

1 pound unsalted butter
1 Granny Smith apple, quartered
  (with core and skin)
1 Winesap apple, quartered (with
  core and skin)
1 Macoun apple, quartered (with core
  and skin)

· Place all ingredients in a heavy,
  4-quart saucepan and cook over
  medium-low to medium heat.
· Simmer for about 30 minutes, low-
  ering the heat as the apples cook
  and stirring occasionally.
· Force through a sieve or stainless
  steel strainer. Cool thoroughly and
  refrigerate, covered.

Makes 3 cups.
Preparation time: 45 minutes.

FIVE • DESSERTS

CRAN-APPLE PIE

CRUST:
½ cup cold unsalted butter, cut into
    small pieces
1 cup all-purpose flour
2 tablespoons sugar
pinch of salt

TOPPING:
¼ cup cold unsalted butter, cut into
    small pieces
½ cup all-purpose flour
⅓ cup light brown sugar

FILLING:
¼ cup fresh or frozen cranberries
4–5 Red Delicious apples, peeled,
    cored and coarsely chopped
¼ cup sugar
pinch of salt

- Preheat oven to 350°.
- Combine crust ingredients in a
  bowl and mix together with your
  fingertips, breaking up butter until
  mixture has the consistency of
  coarse bread crumbs. Add 2 to 3
  tablespoons cold water to bind, and
  form into a patty. Refrigerate for
  30 minutes.
- Combine butter and flour for top-
  ping with fingertips, breaking butter into small, pea-sized pieces. Stir
  in brown sugar, allowing some
  lumps to remain. Set aside.
- Combine filling ingredients and set
  aside.
- Roll dough out into a circle and
  press into a 9-inch pie tin.
- Fill pastry-lined tin with apple-
  cranberry mixture and sprinkle top-
  ping over all.
- Bake 50 minutes to 1 hour, until
  pastry is golden brown. Let cool
  before serving.

Serves 6.
Preparation time: 1 hour 45 minutes.

CALVADOS SOUFFLÉ

1 tablespoon unsalted butter
1 Golden Delicious apple, peeled,
  cored and finely chopped
pinch of salt
4 eggs, separated
⅓ cup sugar
¼ cup calvados

- Preheat oven to 350°.
- Grease four 6-ounce soufflé cups
  with butter and refrigerate.
- Toss apple with salt in a large bowl.
  Set aside until juices form at the
  bottom of the bowl.
- Combine egg yolks, sugar and calvados and set aside.
- Whisk egg whites in a dry bowl
  until stiff peaks form.
- Add a little of the beaten egg white
  to the yolk mixture, then a bit
  more. Very gently fold the entire
  yolk mixture into the remaining
  whites until completely incorporated. Carefully fold in the apple
  and its juices.
- Pour batter into the buttered soufflé
  cups.
- Place the soufflé cups in a 2-inch-
  deep baking tray filled with enough
  water to immerse the cups about ¾
  of the way to their tops.
- Bake for about 12 to 15 minutes,
  until tops have risen about half an
  inch above the rims of the cups. It
  might take a few tries to know ex-
  actly when to take the soufflés out
  of the oven—don't overcook!

Serves 4.
Preparation time: 45 minutes.

JONATHAN APPLES POACHED IN RED WINE

4 Jonathan apples
1½ cups flavorful red wine such as
    Bordeaux or Burgundy
2 teaspoons honey

· Peel the apples, leaving a little skin at the top. With a small spoon, scoop out the core from the bottom. This will allow the apples to poach evenly.
· In a saucepan, heat the wine to a low simmer. Place the apples in the wine, skin side up. Cook for about 20 minutes. When a small knife or toothpick can be inserted easily, remove the apples.
· If the wine is greatly reduced, add about 2 teaspoons of water along with the honey. Heat until the honey has dissolved. Again, if the sauce is too thick, add a little water; if it is too thin, allow to cook down more. Spoon the sauce over the apples.

Serves 4.
Preparation time: 30 minutes.

MACINTOSH APPLE COBBLERS WITH VANILLA ICE CREAM

4 MacIntosh apples, peeled, cored
 and cut into large pieces
¼ cup sugar
pinch of salt
½ cup cold unsalted butter, cut into
 small pieces
¾ cup all-purpose flour
½ cup light brown sugar
1 pint vanilla ice cream

· Preheat oven to 350°.
· Toss apples, sugar and salt together.
 Divide equally among 4 individual
 ovenproof bowls, ramekins or gratin
 dishes.
· Combine butter and flour with fingertips until mixture is crumbly
 and has the texture of oatmeal. Add
 brown sugar, allowing lumps to remain in mixture. Distribute evenly
 over apples.
· Bake 30 minutes. Serve warm or
 cold with a scoop of vanilla ice
 cream.

Serves 4.
Preparation time: 45 minutes.

WINESAP APPLE PUDDING

¾ cup bourbon
1 cup sugar
¼ teaspoon ground nutmeg
½ teaspoon ground cloves
2 teaspoons ground cinnamon
5 eggs
1 quart heavy cream
2 teaspoons unsalted butter
10 slices white bread, crusts trimmed
½ cup raisins
2 Winesap apples, peeled, cored and
  chopped

· Preheat oven to 350°.
· Combine bourbon, sugar, spices, eggs and cream. Set aside.
· Grease a 6-inch-deep loaf pan with the butter.
· Arrange 2½ slices of bread on bottom of loaf pan. Cover with one third of the raisins and apple pieces. Arrange 2½ more slices; cover with more raisins and apples. Repeat a third time until all of the ingredients are used up. Don't place any raisins or apples on the top layer of bread.
· Pour bourbon mixture over bread until it is all absorbed. Bake for about 1 hour, until firm. Cool overnight and serve cold or warm.

Serves 8.
Preparation time: 1 hour 20 minutes, set overnight.

CANDIED
LADY APPLES

1½ cups sugar
6 Lady apples

· In a heavy saucepan, boil sugar and
4 tablespoons water for 3 to 4
minutes.
· To test when sugar is ready, take a
bit of boiling mixture and drop it
into a glass of cold water. If the
sugar forms a hard ball it's ready. If
it forms a soft ball that you can
mold with your fingers after being
dropped in the water, cook for a few
more minutes. (A candy thermome-
ter should read 250°.)
· Make sure apples are thoroughly
washed and dried. Poke a stick into
each apple and dip apples into the
hot sugar mixture. Place directly
onto wax paper and let cool.

Serves 6.
Preparation time: 15 minutes.

GRANNY SMITH APPLE SORBET

6 Granny Smith apples, peeled and
   cored
⅔ cup lemon juice, lime juice or a
   combination of both
⅓ cup sugar
⅓ cup calvados or applejack

· Slice 5 of the apples and puree in a
  blender or food processor. Chop the
  sixth apple finely.
· Combine all ingredients and whisk
  together until sugar is dissolved.
· Pour into 1½-quart (or larger) electric or hand-operated ice cream
  maker. Process until firm following
  manufacturer's instructions.
· Serve immediately or freeze for later
  use.

Serves 6.
Preparation time: 30 minutes to
1 hour.

GOLDEN DELICIOUS APPLE AND CINNAMON ICE CREAM

2 Golden Delicious apples, peeled,
    cored and chopped
1 quart heavy cream
5 egg yolks
1 cup sugar
2 tablespoons vanilla extract
2 teaspoons ground cinnamon (or to
    taste)

· Combine all ingredients in a bowl.
  Whisk together until smooth and
  sugar has dissolved.
· Pour mixture into a 2-quart (or
  larger) electric or hand-operated ice
  cream maker. Process until firm following manufacturer's instructions.
· Serve immediately or freeze for later
  use.

Serves 8.
Preparation time: 30 minutes to
1 hour.

MACOUN APPLE PIE

CRUST:
1 cup cold unsalted butter, cut into
  small pieces
2 cups all-purpose flour
2 tablespoons sugar
pinch of salt
1 egg

FILLING:
5 Macoun apples, peeled, cored and
  thinly sliced
¼ cup sugar (or less if you prefer)
pinch of salt

- Preheat oven to 350°.
- With your fingertips, combine butter, flour, sugar and salt until butter
  is almost entirely incorporated in
  the flour. Allow some butter pieces
  (the size of a lentil or smaller) to remain; this will promote flakiness
  when the pastry is baked. Add 4 to
  5 tablespoons cold water to bind,
  and form dough into a patty. Refrigerate for 30 minutes.
- Combine filling ingredients and set
  aside.
- Roll out half of the dough using ad-
  ditional flour to dust the tabletop,
  and press into a 9-inch pie tin.
- Fill the pastry-lined tin with the
  apple mixture, packing tightly.
- Roll out the remaining dough and
  cut into ¾-inch-wide strips. Arrange strips in a crisscross pattern
  over the apples. When the entire
  pie is covered, trim and press the
  edges together.
- Beat the egg with 2 tablespoons
  cold water. With a brush or fingertips spread the egg wash on the
  dough strips and on the edges.
- Bake 50 minutes to 1 hour, until
  crust is golden brown.
- Cool with a cloth on top to prevent
  the filling from retracting too far
  from the crust.

Serves 6.
Preparation time: 1 hour 45 minutes.

GOLDEN DELICIOUS APPLES WITH CARAMEL AND COOKIES

COOKIES:

7 tablespoons unsalted butter,
 softened
6 tablespoons sugar
¼ teaspoon vanilla extract
¾ cup all-purpose flour
pinch of salt

CARAMEL:

¼ cup sugar
¼ cup heavy cream
⅓ cup unsalted butter, softened

APPLES:

2 Golden Delicious apples, cored
¼ cup chopped pecans (optional)

- Preheat oven to 350°.
- To make cookie dough, combine 6 tablespoons butter with the sugar and vanilla until smooth. Add flour and salt. Mix until dough forms a ball. Roll into a log and refrigerate.
- When the dough is firm cut into 8 equal slices.
- Grease a cookie sheet with the remaining butter. Place the slices of dough on the cookie sheet and bake for 8 to 10 minutes until the edges turn brown. Cool.
- To make caramel, cook the sugar and 2 tablespoons water in a heavy saucepan for about 8 to 10 minutes over medium heat, until golden brown and bubbly—don't burn the sugar!
- Lower heat and slowly add the heavy cream, stirring constantly with a whisk.
- After all the cream is added cook for about 2 to 3 minutes. Remove from heat and stir in butter a little at a time.
- Slice apples thinly and arrange over cookies on 4 plates. Pour hot caramel on top. Sprinkle with chopped nuts if desired.

Serves 4.
Preparation time: 1 hour.

BAKED ROME APPLES WITH COINTREAU

2 Rome apples, peeled and cored
1–1½ cups Cointreau liqueur

· Preheat oven to 350°.
· Place the apples and the liqueur in an ovenproof skillet or saucepan.
· Bake for 1 hour, basting every 10 to 15 minutes.

Serves 2.
Preparation time: 1 hour.

JONATHAN APPLE DUMPLINGS

1 tablespoon butter
2 cups all-purpose flour
pinch of salt
3 tablespoons sugar
1 tablespoon baking powder
¾ cup cold unsalted butter, cut into
    small pieces
½ cup buttermilk
3 Jonathan apples, peeled, cored and
    quartered

· Preheat oven to 350°.
· Grease a cookie sheet with the
  tablespoon of butter.
· Combine flour, salt, 2 tablespoons
  sugar and the baking powder. Mix
  in cold butter with your fingertips.
  Add the buttermilk and work into a
  dough.
· Roll out the dough and cut into 12
  circles. Place an apple quarter on
  each piece of dough, fold the dough
  over the apples and pinch closed.
  Sprinkle remaining sugar over the
  dumplings. Place on greased cookie
  sheet and bake 35 to 40 minutes,
  until golden brown.

Serves 6.
Preparation time: 1 hour.

EMPIRE APPLE AND PEAR TARTS

CRUST:
1½ cups all-purpose flour
¾ cup cold unsalted butter, cut into small pieces
1–2 tablespoons sugar
pinch of salt

FILLING:
½ pound almond paste
3 egg yolks
⅓ cup sugar
½ cup unsalted butter, softened

TOPPING:
2 Empire apples, peeled, cored and thinly sliced
2 pears, peeled, cored and thinly sliced
½ cup raspberry jam mixed with a little water

· Preheat oven to 350°.
· Combine crust ingredients in bowl with fingertips until the consistency of coarse bread crumbs. Add 2 to 3 tablespoons cold water to bind. Form into a ball and refrigerate for 30 minutes.
· Mix all filling ingredients in a blender or food processor.
· Roll out dough and press into four 6-inch-round tart tins. Spread filling on the bottom of each. Arrange apple and pear slices on top of filling. Brush raspberry jam over tops evenly. Bake for 25 to 30 minutes. Cool.

Serves 4.
Preparation time: 1 hour 15 minutes.

SIX • BEVERAGES

APPLE-APRICOT SMOOTHIE

1 Golden Delicious apple, peeled,
  cored and chopped
1 cup apple juice
4 fresh apricots, pitted (skin
  optional)
1 banana, peeled
¾ cup plain yogurt
10–12 ice cubes
1 tablespoon honey

· Place all ingredients in a blender
  and process until smooth.

Serves 2 to 4.
Preparation time: 5 minutes.

APPLE-CRANBERRY ICED TEA

½ cup fresh or frozen cranberries
¼ pound dried apples
1 cinnamon stick
3–4 whole cloves

· Place the cranberries and 1 quart
  cold water in a 2-quart saucepan.
  Bring to a boil.
· Place the apples, cinnamon stick
  and cloves in a 2-quart teapot and
  add the boiling water and
  cranberries.
· Let steep for several minutes and
  strain. Let cool and serve over ice.
  (Also delicious hot!)

Serves 4.
Preparation time: 10 minutes.

HOT BUTTERED CIDER

4 teaspoons unsalted butter
3 ounces dark rum
2 cups apple cider

· Place the butter at the bottom of 2
  mugs. Add half of the rum to each.
· In a small saucepan (or in the microwave) heat the cider until just
  scalded. Pour over the butter and
  rum.

Serves 2.
Preparation time: 5 minutes.

APPLEJACK PUNCH

10–12 ice cubes
4 cups apple cider
1 cup ginger ale
2–3 whole cinnamon sticks
1 cup applejack

· Combine all ingredients in a bowl
  or pitcher. Add the applejack last, a
  little at a time, tasting for desired
  potency.

Serves 6.
Preparation time: 5 minutes.

CALVADOS SPRITZER

8–10 ice cubes
1 cup calvados
2 ounces sparkling water

· Place the ice cubes in 2 tall glasses. Pour the calvados equally into the glasses. Add 1 ounce sparkling water to each, or adjust amount for desired potency.

Serves 2.
Preparation time: 1 minute.

APPLE CIDER SPRITZER

8–10 ice cubes
1½ cups apple cider
2 ounces sparkling water

· Place the ice cubes in 2 tall cocktail glasses. Pour the cider equally into the glasses. Add 1 ounce sparkling water to each, or adjust amount to taste.

Serves 2.
Preparation time: 1 minute.

RECIPE LIST

Apple Cider Spritzer • 116

Apple-Apricot Smoothie • 112

Apple-Cranberry Iced Tea • 112

Apple-Hazelnut Muffins • 20

Applejack Punch • 114

Baked Cortland Apples with Yam
Filling • 50

Baked Rome Apples with
Cointreau • 104

Banana Muffins with Dried Apples
and Apricots • 20

Barbecued Shrimp with Jonathan
Apple and Quince Chutney • 56

Braised Red Cabbage with Northern
Spy Apples • 74

Brook Trout Baked in Parchment
with Northern Spy Apples • 54

Calvados Soufflé • 86

Calvados Spritzer • 116

Candied Lady Apples • 94

Caramelized Greening Apples and
Pearl Onions • 74

Carrot, Parsnip and Granny Smith
Apple Coleslaw • 78

Chicken and Cortland Apple
Couscous • 64

Cracked Wheat Salad with Jonathan
Apples and Mint • 40

Cran-Apple Pie • 84

Duck Breasts with Crab Apples • 62

Empire Apple and Pear Tarts • 108

Fresh Golden Delicious
Apple–Walnut Relish • 76

Ginger Crab Apple Applesauce • 76

Golden Delicious Apple and
Cinnamon Ice Cream • 98

Golden Delicious Apples with
Caramel and Cookies • 102

Granny Smith Apple–Onion Soup
with Celery Root • 34

Granny Smith Apple Sorbet • 96

Greening Apple and Spinach
Pâté • 46

Grilled Swordfish with Lady Apple
Butter • 52

Grilled Veal Chops and Granny
Smith Apples • 70

Hot Buttered Cider • 114

Jonathan Apple Dumplings • 106

Jonathan Apples Poached in Red
Wine • 88

MacIntosh Apple and Blue Cheese
Bisque • 32

MacIntosh Apple and Sausage
Pie • 22

MacIntosh Apple Cobblers with
Vanilla Ice Cream • 90

Macoun Apple Pie • 100

Northern Spy Apple and Butternut
Squash Soup • 30

Northern Spy Apple Fritters • 18

Oatmeal Pancakes with Jonathan
Apples and Pecans • 14

Pork Chops with Rome Apple and
Rosemary Stuffing • 66

Radicchio, Endive and Golden
Delicious Apple Salad • 36

Red Snapper with Empire Apples and
Walnuts • 58

Rome Apple and Goat Cheese
Tartlets • 44

Rome Apple, Orange and Prune
Compote • 16

Smoked Turkey and Gravenstein
Apple Salad • 42

Spareribs with Applesauce Glaze • 68

Spiced Macoun Apple Bread with
Walnuts • 26

Three-Apple Apple Butter • 80

Turkey Potpie with Newtown Pippins
and Onions • 60

Wilted Greens with Red Delicious
Apples and Bacon • 38

Winesap Apple Pudding • 92

Winesap Apple Turnovers • 24

RECIPE LIST BY APPLE OR APPLE PRODUCT

APPLEJACK
Applejack Punch • 114

APPLESAUCE
Spareribs with Applesauce Glaze • 68

CALVADOS
Calvados Soufflé • 86

Calvados Spritzer • 116

CIDER
Apple Cider Spritzer · 116
Applejack Punch · 114
Hot Buttered Cider · 114

CORTLAND
Baked Cortland Apples with Yam
Filling · 50
Chicken and Cortland Apple
Couscous · 64

CRAB APPLES
Duck Breasts with Crab Apples · 62
Ginger Crab Apple Applesauce · 76

DRIED APPLES
Apple-Cranberry Iced Tea · 112
Apple-Hazelnut Muffins · 20
Banana Muffins with Dried Apples
and Apricots · 20

EMPIRE
Empire Apple and Pear Tarts · 108
Red Snapper with Empire Apples and
Walnuts · 58

GOLDEN DELICIOUS
Apple-Apricot Smoothie · 112
Fresh Golden Delicious
Apple–Walnut Relish · 76
Golden Delicious Apple and
Cinnamon Ice Cream · 98
Golden Delicious Apples with
Caramel and Cookies · 102
Radicchio, Endive and Golden
Delicious Apple Salad · 36

GRANNY SMITH
Carrot, Parsnip and Granny Smith
Apple Coleslaw · 78
Granny Smith Apple–Onion Soup
with Celery Root · 34

Granny Smith Apple Sorbet · 96
Grilled Veal Chops and Granny
Smith Apples · 70
Three-Apple Apple Butter · 80

GRAVENSTEIN
Smoked Turkey and Gravenstein
Apple Salad · 42

GREENING
Caramelized Greening Apples and
Pearl Onions · 74
Greening Apple and Spinach
Pâté · 46

JONATHAN
Barbecued Shrimp with Jonathan
Apple and Quince Chutney · 56
Cracked Wheat Salad with Jonathan
Apples and Mint · 40
Jonathan Apple Dumplings · 106
Jonathan Apples Poached in Red
Wine · 88
Oatmeal Pancakes with Jonathan
Apples and Pecans · 14

JUICE
Apple-Apricot Smoothie · 112

LADY APPLES
Candied Lady Apples · 94
Grilled Swordfish with Lady Apple
Butter · 52

MACOUN
Macoun Apple Pie · 100
Spiced Macoun Apple Bread with
Walnuts · 26
Three-Apple Apple Butter · 80

MACINTOSH
MacIntosh Apple and Blue Cheese
Bisque · 32
MacIntosh Apple and Sausage
Pie · 22
MacIntosh Apple Cobblers with
Vanilla Ice Cream · 90

NEWTOWN PIPPINS
Turkey Potpie with Newtown Pippins
and Onions · 60

NORTHERN SPY
Braised Red Cabbage with Northern
Spy Apples · 74
Brook Trout Baked in Parchment
with Northern Spy Apples · 54
Northern Spy Apple and Butternut
Squash Soup · 30
Northern Spy Apple Fritters · 18

RED DELICIOUS
Cran-Apple Pie · 84
Wilted Greens with Red Delicious
Apples and Bacon · 38

ROME
Baked Rome Apples with
Cointreau · 104
Pork Chops with Rome Apple and
Rosemary Stuffing · 66
Rome Apple and Goat Cheese
Tartlets · 44
Rome Apple, Orange and Prune
Compote · 16

WINESAP
Three-Apple Apple Butter · 80
Winesap Apple Pudding · 92
Winesap Apple Turnovers · 24

SOURCES

The hundreds of orchards where you can pick your own fruit are great sources for the freshest apples. Most states in the northern half of the U.S. and a few in the South have "you-pick" orchards; to find those nearest you, contact your state's agricultural extension service or department of agriculture.

Another good source of apples, apple products and just plain fun is the many apples festivals held throughout the U.S., usually in the fall. Contact your state's department of tourism or chamber of commerce for dates and locations.

The following is a list of suppliers from whom fresh apples and apple products can be obtained by phone or mail order. Call or write for individual catalogues or price lists, shipping costs and procedures and availability of products.

Cherry Hill Cooperative Cannery
M.R. 1
Barre, VT 05641
(802) 479-2558
Applesauces; apple butters; apple cider jelly.

The Children's Catalog
Children's Home Society of
    Washington
P.O. Box 15190
Seattle, WA 98115-0190
(800) 456-3338
(206) 523-5727
Fresh Red Delicious and Granny Smith apples. Proceeds benefit the society.

Cold Hollow Cider Mill
Route 100, Box 430
Waterbury Center, VT 05677
(800) 3-APPLES
(800) U-C-CIDER in VT
Fresh MacIntosh apples; cider jelly; cider concentrate; cider syrup; applesauces; apple butters; apple blossom honey.

Dean & DeLuca
Mail Order Department
560 Broadway
New York, NY 10012
(800) 221-7714
(212) 431-1691
Plain and flavored cider vinegars.

F.H. Gillingham & Company
16 Elm Street
Woodstock, VT 05091
(802) 457-2100
A hand-operated machine that peels, cores and slices apples in one step.

Grafton Village Apple Company, Inc.
RR 3, Box 236D
Grafton, VT 05146
(800) 843-4822
(802) 843-2406
Fresh MacIntosh, Cortland and Crispin apples; apple preserves; apple jelly; cider syrup; applesauces; apple butters.

Hadley Fruit Orchards
P.O. Box 495
Cabazon, CA 92230
(800) 854-5655
(800) 472-5672 in CA
Sulphured and unsulphured dried apples; sugar-free apple butter.

Jaffe Bros. Inc.
P.O. Box 636
Valley Center, CA 92082-0636
(619) 749-1133
Unsulphured dried apples; apple juices; apple butters. All organic.

Kitchen Kettle Village
Box 380
Intercourse, PA 17534
(800) 732-3538
(717) 768-8261
Applesauce; apple butter; apple-pepper chutney; apple jellies. Some available sugar free.

Kozlowski Farms
5566 Gravenstein Highway
Forestville, CA 95436
(707) 887-1587
Applesauces; apple butter; cider jelly; cider syrup; apple chutney; cider vinegar. Many available organic and sugar free.

Pinnacle Orchards
441 South Fir Street
Medford, OR 97501-0077
(800) 547-0227
Fresh Red Delicious apples.

R&R Mill Company, Inc.
Smithfield Implement Company
45 West First North
Smithfield, VT 84335
(801) 563-3333
Dehydrators for making dried apples at home.

Timber Crest Farms
4791 Dry Creek Road
Healdsburg, CA 95448
(707) 433-8251
Dried Golden Delicious apples; sugar-free apple butter. All organic and unsulphured, available in small quantity or bulk.

Walnut Acres
Penns Creek, PA 17862
(800) 433-3998
Dried apples; cider vinegar; applesauce; apple juice; apple butter; pectin. All organic and unsulphured.